A World of Food

LEBANON

Cath Senker

W
FRANKLIN WATTS
LONDON • SYDNEY

First published in 2010 by Franklin Watts

Copyright © 2010 Arcturus Publishing Limited

Franklin Watts
338 Euston Road
London NW1 3BH

Franklin Watts Australia
Level 17/207 Kent Street, Sydney, NSW 2000

Produced by Arcturus Publishing Limited,
26/27 Bickels Yard, 151–153 Bermondsey Street, London SE1 3HA

Series concept: Alex Woolf
Editor: Alex Woolf
Designer: Jane Hawkins
Map illustrator: Stefan Chabluk
Picture researcher: Alex Woolf

Picture Credits
Amy Dreher: 21 *right*.
Art Archive: 6 (Topkapi Museum, Istanbul/Alfredo Dagli Orti), 11 (W Robert Moore/NGS Image Collection).
Corbis: 9 (Ivan Vdovin/JAI), 13 (Roger Wood), 19 (Jamal Saidi/Reuters), 20 (Wael Hamzeh/epa), 21 *left* (Wael Hamzeh/epa), 28 (Thomas Hartwell).
Cyclone Bill: 15 *tabbouleh*.
Getty Images: cover (Joseph Barrak/AFP), 7 (Stan Wayman/Time & Life Pictures), 8 (Joseph Barrak/AFP), 10 (Ramzi Haidar/AFP), 12 (Win Initiative), 14 (Joseph Barrak/AFP) 16 (Courtney Kealy), 18 (Mahmoud Zayat/AFP), 24 (Courtney Kealy), 25 (Thomas J Abercrombie/National Geographic), 26 (Brigitte Stelzer).
Linda Kovacevic: 27 *muhallabia*.
Nora Staal: 22.
Rex Features: 4, 29 (Tony Kyriacou).
Shutterstock: 15 *bulgur wheat* (Jovan Nikolic), 15 *parsley and mint* (Bienchen-s), 15 *lemons and tomatoes* (Tatiana Popova), 15 *olive oil* (ilker canikligil), 17 (najmu), 23 *yoghurt* (angelo gilardelli), 23 *flour* (Le Loft 1911), 23 *cinnamon* (Ariy), 23 *honey* (Julián Rovagnati), 27 *salt* (Joseph Calev), 27 *milk* (Jozsef Szasz-Fabian), 27 *almond flour* (Olga Lyubkina), 27 *pistachios* (Bienchen-s).
Spencer James: 23 *awwamaat*.

Cover picture: A mezze is served at a restaurant in Antelias, a suburb of Beirut, Lebanon.

Every attempt has been made to clear copyright. Should there be any inadvertent omission, please apply to the publisher for rectification.

Acknowledgements
The author would like to acknowledge the following sources: *Arabesque: A Taste of Morocco, Turkey and Lebanon* by Claudia Roden (Knopf, 2006) for some of the historical background; recipe on pages 22–23 from http://foodgeeks.com; recipe on pages 26–27 adapted from RecipeZaar.

A CIP catalogue record for this book is available from the British Library.

Dewey Decimal Classification Number: 394.1'2'095692

ISBN 978 0 7496 9360 2

Printed in China

Franklin Watts is a division of Hachette Children's Books, an Hachette UK company.
www.hachette.co.uk

Contents

Introduction

Lebanon is a small country in the Middle East, about half of the size of Wales. To the west is the Mediterranean Sea, to the east is Syria, and to the south is Israel.

The people of Lebanon

In Lebanon, about 60 per cent of the population are Muslim, while about 40 per cent are Christian. There are several different Muslim and Christian groups. The main language spoken is Arabic.

The majority of the people live in the coastal cities of Beirut, Tripoli, Sidon and Tyre. Other regions, particularly Al-Biqa Valley, have a sparse population. Lebanon has a young population. More than half of the people are under 30, and nearly one-third are under 15!

▲ Young women relax in a Beirut cafe. The woman on the left enjoys freshly squeezed fruit juice.

Tastes of Lebanon

Lebanese food is extremely varied because Lebanon has been influenced by many countries over history. In addition, it has three climate zones, where different foods grow.

Today, Lebanese cuisine is known around the world for its mezze dishes – a wonderful range of snacks eaten as a starter. Mezze foods include little meat pizzas and spinach pies, made from a light puff pastry and stuffed with lemony spinach. Also on a mezze table will be hummus, aubergine dip and tabbouleh (bulgur wheat salad).

For their main meal, people enjoy hearty plates of stuffed vegetables, fish or *kibbe* – small meat and bulgur-wheat pies. These dishes are served with rice or bulgur wheat. The Lebanese love their desserts, which they sweeten with special flower flavourings – orange blossom water and rose water. Some favourites are milk pudding, and ice cream with rose water.

SOME COMMON LEBANESE FOODS

Word	Pronunciation	Meaning
khobz	*khubz* (kh as in 'loch')	bread
laban	LAA-ban	yogurt
labne	LAB-neh	soft cheese
rooz	ruz	rice
zayt	zayt	olive oil
zaytoon	zay-TOON	olives

▶ This map of Lebanon shows many of the places mentioned in this book.

History of Food

Lebanese cuisine is a mixture of food traditions. Owing to Lebanon's location, it has many Mediterranean features. It is also heavily influenced by the cooking traditions of the Islamic world.

Each empire that ruled Lebanon brought new dishes to the kitchen. In the seventh century, the new Islamic empire gained control of the region. In the ninth century, rulers based in Egypt took over. They brought dishes such as falafel – spicy chickpea balls.

In the 16th century, the Ottoman Empire (based in Turkey) seized control. The Ottoman Turks introduced foods that became staples of the Lebanese diet. They brought stuffed vegetables and baklava – sweet pastries made with honey and nuts.

Because of its position on the Mediterranean coast, Lebanon has always been a trading centre. Spices were imported from Far Eastern lands and used to add a variety of flavours to dishes.

◀ An Ottoman Turkish ruler eating a picnic, 1520. There is a strong Turkish influence on Lebanese food.

Mezze

The mezze tradition began around 1920 in Al-Biqa Valley. At that time, some cafes opened by the riverside in the holiday town of Zahle. The staff offered their customers tasty snacks to eat with their drinks. There were olives, nuts, raw vegetables and pieces of cheese. Serving mezze developed into the favourite way to entertain guests in Lebanon.

▲ This photo from 1961 shows a vast array of mezze dishes served in a Lebanese restaurant.

French food

A new influence came with French rule over Lebanon (1920–46). The French introduced their own foods, including croissants and *flan* (crème caramel), a dessert made from sugar, milk, eggs and vanilla.

Healthy eating

The latest influence on eating habits has been the change in people's lifestyles. Now, especially in towns and cities, people have less time to spend in the kitchen. They are concerned about eating healthily. Lebanese cuisine has adapted to these changes.

COOKING

In the past, Lebanese people cooked outdoors using wood-burning clay ovens. In many communities they went to a shared public oven to cook. Nowadays, people use modern cookers.

Climate and Soil

The climate and soil affect the kinds of food that farmers can grow. Lebanon has three different climate zones: the coastal area, the mountains and Al-Biqa Valley.

Climate

The climate is so varied that for most of the year, you could swim in the sea at the coast and go skiing in the mountains on the same day! The narrow coastal area has a Mediterranean climate. Winters are cool and wet. Summers are hot and humid, with little rain. There is heavy dew, which is good for crops.

In the mountain areas, dense snow falls during the winter. The peaks of the Lebanon Mountains and the Anti-Lebanon Mountains are covered in snow for much of the year. During the summer, it is hot during the day but the temperature drops sharply at night.

In Al-Biqa Valley, summers are hot and dry. Winters are cold with severe north winds, but there is less rain than elsewhere in the country.

▶ Winter snow in Bhamdoun, a town about 20km east of Beirut, on Mount Lebanon. Mountain towns like Bhamdoun are popular with tourists in summer because temperatures are cooler than in the coastal cities.

KHAMSIN

During the spring, a hot wind blows from the Egyptian desert. It is called the *khamsin* – the Arabic word for 'fifty' – because it normally blows for about 50 days of the year. The *khamsin* can raise the temperature to a baking 40°C, or even higher. The wind carries vast amounts of sand and dust, causing sandstorms.

▼ A view of Al-Biqa Valley. The valley contains half of the country's land that is suitable for farming.

Rainfall and water

Lebanon has plenty of rain, which mostly falls in the winter rainy season. Many rivers, streams and springs provide water for farming and people's needs.

Soil

In the higher mountain areas, the shallow limestone soil is poor, so it is impossible to cultivate crops. The lower and middle slopes have rich enough soil for farming. The northern mountains and the narrow sea coast have fertile soil containing clay. The clay holds in moisture and is good for growing crops, but these areas suffer from soil erosion. In the east, Al-Biqa Valley has extremely fertile soils.

Farming

In Lebanon, farmers can grow a variety of European and tropical crops. Different crops are raised in the mountains, valleys and on the coast.

A land of trees

On the middle slopes of the mountains, apple and pear trees grow. On the lower slopes, farmers tend peach, plum, apricot and cherry trees. Along the coastal plain, people grow bananas and citrus fruit, as well as vegetables.

▲ This man in southern Lebanon throws a sack of fresh olives into a mill to turn them into olive oil.

Olive trees are found in many regions of Lebanon. Around 40 per cent of olive groves are in the north. About one-third of the olives are eaten fresh, while two-thirds are turned into olive oil, which is used in all Lebanese cooking.

Cereals and herbs

In Al-Biqa Valley, farmers cultivate cereals such as wheat and barley, vegetables, and grapevines for grapes and winemaking. Around Jubayl, near Beirut, avocados are grown.

Lebanese food is always well seasoned. Farmers harvest herbs in the mountains. Some of the most popular are *zaatar* (a herb rather like thyme) and sumac, a sour spice that can be used instead of lemon.

Livestock

Many Lebanese farmers keep livestock, especially poultry, sheep, goats and cattle. They raise more poultry than any other kind of animal. Cows and goats are kept for their milk, which is made into *laban* and *labne*. Along the coast, many kinds of fish are available to enrich people's diets.

PRESERVING PRODUCE

In rural areas, Lebanese people traditionally preserved food to last through the winter. This winter store was called the *mune*. Farmers dried fruit in the sun, preserved meats and made fruit and vegetables into jams and pickles. They preserved olives in oil, clarified butter and made yogurt and cheese. To flavour their desserts, they distilled rose and orange blossom waters. During the civil war in Lebanon (1975–90), the *mune* tradition was revived because it was hard to buy food.

► These fruit farmers from Baalbek in the Al-Biqa Valley lay out sheets of apricot paste to dry in the sun.

Culture

In Lebanese culture it is important to welcome guests with mezze or cakes. Yet family meals are normally based on meat and rice. Food traditions in Lebanon are changing, particularly in the cities.

▲ This family is sharing the evening meal in the traditional way. In some places, people sit on the floor when they eat and use their hands.

It is a great Arab tradition to offer refreshments to guests who turn up at any time of the day. If you visit a Lebanese family, you will probably be offered a tray of mezze. If you arrive in the afternoon, you may be treated to coffee and baklava.

How people eat

In Lebanon, all the dishes are laid out on the table and everyone helps themselves. People eat with their fingers, but always with the right hand. In Islam, using the left hand to eat is thought to be unclean. To eat mezze, you pick up food with a piece of bread or dip it into the dishes. You can also roll up your bread and fill it with food.

BREAD

Bread is a staple food, eaten with most meals. The most common type is *markouk*, which is like a giant, thin pancake. *Khobz halabi* (Aleppo bread) is a thin pitta bread. *Kaak bil simsum* (sesame bread) is a ring of bread sprinkled with sesame seeds. It is sold on the streets as a snack.

Families at home normally eat one dish for their main lunchtime meal rather than mezze. They often eat meat or vegetable stew, or stuffed vegetables, served with rice or bulgur wheat. Alongside the main dish, people enjoy a mixed salad or fresh vegetables, such as radishes or cucumber.

City ways

In cities, working life makes it hard for families to sit down to a large, home-cooked lunch every day. Lebanese cities have many restaurants and cafes. City dwellers eat out more than rural people and cook less at home.

◄ On this table, there is plenty of *khobz halabi* for dipping into the *labne* (top left), hummus (bottom left) and aubergine dip (bottom right).

Christian Influence

Christian customs have had an important influence on Lebanon's national cuisine. Traditionally, Christians ate no meat during periods of fasting, and a wealth of vegetarian dishes exist.

Fast foods

Lebanese Christians have many fasts. Until a few decades ago, they followed these fasts strictly. They could not eat food from animals (sometimes including dairy products and eggs) for several periods. These included 40 days before Christmas, during Lent, and every Wednesday and Friday. At these times, people cooked meals with pulses such as chickpeas and lentils to provide protein. Vegetarian dishes such as tabbouleh and spinach pies were commonly eaten during fasts.

▼ Christians are permitted to drink alcohol, and Lebanon produces many fine wines. Here, a farm worker loads a huge bucket of grapes into a truck at a vineyard in Al-Biqa Valley.

RECIPE: tabbouleh

Equipment
- bowl   • tea towel   • sharp knife   • chopping board   • wooden spoon

Ingredients (serves 6)
- 75g fine-ground bulgur wheat
- juice of 2 lemons
- 5 tablespoons olive oil
- 250g bunch of flat-leaf parsley
- 50g fresh mint
- 400g tomatoes, diced
- 6 spring onions, sliced thinly
- salt and black pepper to taste
- 1 Cos or 2 Little Gem lettuces

Ask a grown-up to help you with the slicing and dicing.

1 Place the bulgur wheat in a bowl and cover with boiling water. Leave for about 15 minutes, until the grains are soft. Allow to cool.

2 Mix the bulgur wheat with the lemon juice and olive oil. Set aside.

3 Keep the parsley in its bunch. Wash it. Shake the water out and dry it on a clean tea towel.

4 Slice the parsley finely with a sharp knife.

5 Wash the mint. Pick off the leaves and slice them finely.

6 Add the mint and parsley to the bulgur wheat.

7 Just before serving, add the diced tomatoes, spring onions, salt and pepper. Cut the Cos lettuce leaves in half or separate the Little Gem lettuce leaves. Put the lettuce in a bowl.

8 Eat the tabbouleh by scooping it up with the lettuce leaves

Muslim Influence

Muslim traditions have also affected Lebanese cooking. Since Muslims eat no meat from the pig, poultry and lamb are the favourite meats. Muslims do not drink alcohol, but they enjoy a wide range of delicious non-alcoholic drinks.

Meat dishes

The Lebanese eat chicken more often than red meat. Chicken dishes are usually strongly flavoured, with plenty of garlic and lemon juice. When people eat red meat, it is normally lamb, although goat meat is eaten in the mountain areas. Lamb is often served sliced in *shawarma* (see page 26) or minced and made into meatballs or *kibbe*.

Drinks

Coffee drinking is common in all Muslim countries. People often drink coffee throughout the day. All visitors are offered a cup, however short their visit. In Lebanon, coffee is served strong and thick, with several spoonfuls of sugar. Often, a spice called cardamom is added for flavour. Mint tea is another typical drink offered to guests. It is made with green tea, fresh mint leaves and lots of sugar.

The Lebanese make syrups from fruits such as dates, grapes and apricots, which are mixed with water to make a refreshing drink. A hot milky drink called *sahlab* is also popular. It is thickened with a powder made from the dried root of an orchid.

Sweets

As well as sweetened drinks, the Lebanese are known for their sweet foods. The custom of making rich cakes, biscuits and baklava is linked to the Muslim festival of Id ul-Fitr, at the end of Ramadan (see pages 18–19).

COFFEE

It is the custom to make Lebanese coffee in a special long-handled pot called a *rakweh*. Drinking coffee is part of the culture in Lebanon. There is a joke that a Lebanese person who does not drink coffee might lose their Lebanese nationality!

▼ A plate with various delicious kinds of baklava. Sweets like these are eaten in many Muslim countries.

◄ A waiter serves coffee from a traditional long-handled coffee pot. Lebanese people drink a large amount of coffee.

Muslim Celebrations

All the major Muslim and Christian festivals are celebrated in Lebanon. The key Muslim festivals are Id ul-Fitr, at the end of Ramadan, and Id ul-Adha. For Christians, Easter and Christmas are the most significant celebrations.

The main Muslim festivals

During the Muslim month of Ramadan, Muslims neither eat nor drink during the daylight hours. The purpose is to focus on God. At Id ul-Fitr, people celebrate the end of the fast.

At Id ul-Adha, Muslims remember how Ibrahim was prepared to kill his own son to show his faith in God. God did not make him do it, but Ibrahim had shown his strong faith. In Lebanon, there are two-day public holidays for both Id ul-Fitr and Id ul-Adha.

▲ Lebanese families at a restaurant in Tyre eat the early breakfast meal before dawn in Ramadan. During Ramadan, families and friends like to gather together for meals.

Ramadan

During this month, Muslims eat their main meal after sunset in the evening. They awake before dawn to eat a light breakfast before the sun rises. In Lebanon, breakfast is often a grapefruit, some flatbread dipped in olive oil and a boiled egg. The food is washed down with a cup of *laban* and some tea.

SWEET TREATS

At Id ul-Fitr, it is traditional to make tasty sweet dishes at home, including milky desserts and cakes. In Lebanon, the most popular are *ma'amul* – date-filled semolina cakes.

Id ul-Fitr

At Id ul-Fitr, Muslims enjoy a special lunch. It is the first main meal they have eaten during the day for a month! On the table are favourite dishes such as lamb *kibbe*, roast chicken or stuffed vegetables, and rice.

Id ul-Adha

At this festival, Muslims hold a feast to celebrate Ibrahim's faith. There is usually a large platter of mutton – the meat from a sheep – served with rice. The meat is shared with friends, neighbours and poor people in the community.

◀ Sheep at a market in Beirut two days before Id ul-Adha. Their meat will be eaten at the feast.

Easter

Like Id ul-Fitr, Easter is a festival that follows a period of fasting. For Christians, it is the tradition to avoid food from animals during the 40 days of Lent. They avoid eating butter, milk and eggs. This custom reminds them that Jesus spent 40 days in the desert without food.

◄ A traditional Palm Sunday procession in Beirut, held the week before Easter Sunday.

On Easter Sunday, Christians remember how Jesus rose from the dead after dying on the cross. The miracle showed that life could win over death.

Ma'amul

The *ma'amul* eaten by Christians at Easter are similar to those eaten by Muslims at Id ul-Fitr. A few days before the festival, women in the family gather to make them. They form the dough from semolina and butter and divide it into round or oval shapes. They stuff the *ma'amul* with crushed dates or nuts.

People eat *ma'amul* on Easter Sunday to break their fast. It is the first time they have eaten butter since the start of Lent.

Easter Sunday lunch

On Easter Sunday, families go to church. Afterwards, they gather for a festive lunch with meat. There may be lamb, chicken or turkey stuffed with nuts, and eaten with rice. In the afternoon, people visit friends and family. They go to as many homes as possible. The hosts offer sweet snacks to their guests, laid out on large plates. As well as *ma'amul*, there may be sugar-coated chickpeas and sugared almonds.

THE SHAPES OF MA'AMUL

According to tradition, the Easter *ma'amul* are made into round or oval shapes. The round shape stands for the crown Jesus wore when he was led to the cross. The oval one is a symbol for the sponge given to Jesus so he could squeeze out water to drink. Cooks pinch the surface of the *ma'amul* to stand for the thorns on Jesus' crown.

▲ This is a round version of *ma'amul*. The cakes are served with tea or coffee.

◄ A Lebanese woman examines a collection of Easter eggs on display at a market in Sidon.

Christmas

At Christmas, Christians celebrate the birth of Jesus. They create a Nativity scene with a crib. The biggest celebrations are on Christmas Day.

In Lebanon, people show the Nativity scene in a cave rather than a stable. At least three weeks before Christmas, they plant chickpeas, wheat, beans and lentils in wet cotton wool. When the seeds have sprouted and grown tall, people add the little plants to their Nativity scene.

Christmas Day

On Christmas morning, people visit friends. Their hosts offer them coffee and sugared almonds. At lunch, families gather for a huge meal of chicken, *kibbe* or turkey, with rice. Dessert is often a French Christmas cake like a yule log, called a *bûche de Noël*.

During the Christmas season, people in Lebanon and Syria eat delicious little doughnuts called *awwamaat*.

▲ This Nativity scene in a cave shows the Wise Men visiting baby Jesus. You can see the living plants at the front.

RECIPE: awwamaat

Equipment
- bowl • sieve • frying pan • spatula • kitchen roll • saucepan

Ingredients (for about 24 *awwamaat*)
- 1 cup plain yogurt
- ¼ teaspoon baking powder
- pinch of salt • 1¾ cups flour
- sesame oil for frying

For the honey glaze:
- ½ cup honey
- 1 tablespoon ground cinnamon
- 1 tablespoon lemon juice

1 Beat the yogurt until smooth and thin. Mix with the baking powder and salt.

2 Gradually sift in the flour, using a sieve. Stir until the mixture can barely be dropped from a spoon.

3 Ask a grown-up to heat the oil until it is very hot (190°C).

4 Using two wet teaspoons, drop spoonfuls of dough into the oil.

5 Turn after about 2 minutes when the balls of dough are brown underneath. Fry the other side.

6 Drain the *awwamaat* on the kitchen roll.

Honey glaze

1 Put all the ingredients into a saucepan and bring to the boil.

2 Simmer for one minute. Pour into a bowl.

Dip your warm *awwamaat* in the honey glaze to eat them.

Town and Country Food

Although Lebanon is a small country, each region has its own food traditions. Until the 1960s there were no roads between the coast and the interior, so these regions were isolated from each other. Each area developed its own dishes, depending on the produce that grew locally.

▼ A smart cafe in Beirut. In the towns and cities, it is common to go out for coffee and cakes.

In the towns and cities, rice was traditionally the staple food, eaten at all main meals. In rural parts, people ate bulgur wheat. In the 1960s and early 1970s, the government built roads to link up the different regions of the country. The increase in communication allowed people to learn about food customs in other places. The rice and bulgur wheat traditions combined to form the Lebanese cuisine we know today.

In the cities

Regional differences still exist though, partly owing to differences in wealth. In general, people in Beirut and the other cities along the coast are better off than the people living inland. Urban people have a varied diet and can choose to eat local or international food.

In the countryside

In rural areas, on the other hand, people still mostly live off the land. Many villages have grapevines, olive trees, wheat fields and flocks of sheep and goats. Villagers grow their own vegetables. They grind wheat into flour to make bread and make their own dairy products and olive oil. Most people are poor – they eat mainly vegetarian food and can rarely afford to eat meat.

▼ These women in Al-Biqa Valley make bread in the traditional way, using an oven fuelled with straw.

City Food

All Lebanese cities have countless small cafes where families go to enjoy freshly squeezed fruit juice, strong Arabic coffee and ice cream. *Shawarma* and falafel are common snacks everywhere, but various cities also have their own special dishes.

Street snacks

Shawarma sandwiches are tasty snacks bought from street stalls. *Shawarma* is seasoned meat, cut from a giant skewer and served in pitta bread with tahini (sesame paste), salad and pickles. A vegetarian alternative is falafel, eaten in pitta bread in the same way.

Beirut

In Beirut, the most popular snack made in street-corner bakeries is *manouché*. It is round bread filled or topped with *zaatar*, like a little pizza. The city is also known for *akhtabout* (a spicy dish of fish and octopus) and its high-class French restaurants.

Tripoli – the sweet capital

Tripoli is famous for its sticky Arabic sweets, pastries and ice cream. One special sweet is *halawet al-jibn*, made from soft, chewy cheese and served with syrup.

▶ A man sells *kaak bil simsum* (sesame bread) on the street in Beirut.

Sidon

A speciality of Sidon is a dish of rice and fava beans (broad beans). Sidon is also known for its Arabic sweets and a crumbly biscuit called *seniora*.

RECIPE: muhallabia *(milk pudding)*

This is a much-loved dessert in Lebanon.

Equipment
• bowl • saucepan • wooden spoon

Ingredients
• ¼ cup rice flour • 3 cups milk
• 1 pinch salt • ¼ cup sugar
• ¾ cup ground almonds
• 1 tablespoon rose water (available from Middle Eastern shops)
• pistachios or almonds to garnish (optional)

1 Blend the rice flour in ¼ cup of milk.

2 Bring the rest of the milk to the boil. Blend in the rice flour mixture, salt and sugar.

3 Turn to medium-high heat. Stir until the mixture bubbles gently.

4 Simmer for 5 minutes, stirring continually. Turn the heat down if necessary.

5 Add the ground almonds and mix well.

6 Add the rose water.

7 Remove from heat and stir occasionally until the mixture cools slightly.

8 When the pudding is cold, put it in the fridge to chill.

9 Serve with nuts on top, if you like.

Global Influences

Lebanese food has been influenced by the cuisines of other lands. Most recently, Western eating styles have affected the Lebanese diet. Lebanese people have opened restaurants in many countries, and their cooking now represents Arab food worldwide.

◄ The McDonald's 'M' and restaurant sign in Arabic tower above the apartment blocks in the coastal city of Jounieh.

New rulers, new foods

Lebanese food is similar to the cuisines of Turkey, Syria, Palestine and Jordan. All of these countries were part of the Islamic empire from the seventh century onwards. Lebanon was later also ruled by Egyptian powers, the Ottoman Empire and France (see pages 6–7). Each of these ruling powers introduced their dishes to Lebanon.

Changing diets

From the 19th century onwards, Lebanese Christians began to migrate to Egypt, France and the Americas for a better life. Many returned home with new customs. They had learned to cook lighter food, using butter and oil instead of clarified butter.

In recent decades, Lebanese people have started to eat Western-style foods, such as pasta, white bread, chips and processed food. Fast-food pizza and burger restaurants have spread in the cities. Owing to the change in diet and a lack of exercise, more and more Lebanese people are overweight.

Mezze around the world

The Lebanese have taken their food customs abroad, too. They were the first people in the Middle East to develop the restaurant trade. From 1958 to 1975, Lebanon enjoyed a period of peace and growing wealth. Better-off people could afford to eat in restaurants. Then, during the civil war in the 1970s and 1980s, large numbers of Lebanese people fled to Europe and the United States. To make a living, many set up Lebanese restaurants. Nowadays, Lebanese food – and especially mezze – represents Arab food to people all around the world.

▶ A Lebanese restaurant on Edgware Road, an area of London known for Middle Eastern food.

BEIRUT – GLOBAL CUISINE

As well as excellent Lebanese restaurants, Beirut has many international eateries. You can enjoy French, Thai, Italian, Greek, Mexican, Japanese food and several other kinds of cuisine.

Glossary

baklava A rich, sweet pastry made from layers of flaky pastry filled with nuts and honey.

bulgur wheat A cereal food made from wheat, which comes in tiny, cracked shapes. You can buy fine, medium or coarse bulgur wheat.

civil war A war between groups of people in the same country. The civil war in Lebanon also involved other countries such as Israel and Syria.

clarified butter A cooking fat made by removing the water and milk solids from butter to leave just the clear fat.

fast Go without food, for example for religious reasons.

fertile Describing land or soil where plants grow well.

hummus A paste made from chickpeas, tahini, olive oil and garlic.

laban Natural yogurt, made at home using a little yogurt and fresh milk.

labne A simple cheese made by draining natural yogurt through muslin, a finely woven cotton fabric.

limestone A type of white stone.

mezze A selection of dishes served as a starter.

orange blossom water A flavouring made by boiling the blossom of the bitter orange tree.

orchid A plant with brightly coloured flowers of unusual shapes.

puff pastry A light, flaky pastry made of many layers.

pulses The seeds of some plants, such as peas and lentils, which are eaten as food.

rose water A flavouring made by boiling rose petals and condensing the steam.

semolina Large, hard grains of wheat that can be used in sweet dishes.

soil erosion The wearing away of the land through natural processes or through the actions of people.

staple A basic food, forming an important part of the diet.

tahini A paste made from crushed sesame seeds.

tropical To do with the tropics, the hottest part of the world.

zaatar A herb like thyme. *Zaatar* is also the name for a seasoning made with ground thyme, oregano and marjoram, toasted sesame seeds, sumac and salt.

Further Information

Books

Arabesque by Claudia Roden (Michael Joseph, 2005)

Cooking the Lebanese Way by Suad Amari (Lerner Publications, 2006)

Countries in Crisis: Lebanon by James Stewart (Rourke Publishing, 2008)

Cultures of the World: Lebanon by Sean Sheehan and Zawiah Abdul Latif (Marshall Cavendish, 2007)

The Lebanese Kitchen: Quick and Healthy Recipes by Monique Bassila Zaarour (Interlink Books, 2008)

Websites

www.easy-kids-recipes.com/lebanese-recipes.html
Easy Kids' Recipes: Lebanese recipes for main meals and snacks.

www.foodbycountry.com/Kazakhstan-to-South-Africa/Lebanon.html
Food in Lebanon: General information about Lebanon, and recipes.

www.monkeysee.com/play/1548-lebanese-recipes
Monkey See: Watch a chef making Lebanese dishes.

www.recipezaar.com/browse/top/236
Recipe Zaar: Popular Lebanese recipes.

Index